MONSTERS & MYTHS
FEROCIOUS GIANTS

By Gerrie McCall and Lisa Regan

Gareth Stevens
Publishing

D1591882

Please visit our Web site, www.garethstevens.com. For a free color catalog of all our high-quality books, call toll free 1-800-542-2595 or fax 1-877-542-2596.

Library of Congress Cataloging-in-Publication Data

McCall, Gerrie.
Ferocious giants / Gerrie McCall and Lisa Regan.
    p. cm. — (Monsters & myths)
ISBN 978-1-4339-5000-1 (library binding)
ISBN 978-1-4339-5001-8 (pbk.)
ISBN 978-1-4339-5002-5 (6-pack)
1. Giants. 2. Animals, Mythical. I. Regan, Lisa. II. Title.
GN69.M33 2011
398.24'54—dc22

                              2010039133

Published in 2011 by
Gareth Stevens Publishing
111 East 14th Street, Suite 349
New York, NY 10003

Printed in the United States of America

CPSIA compliance information: Batch #CW11GS: For further information contact Gareth Stevens, New York, New York at 1-800-542-2595.

Table of Contents

Azhi Dahaka

FACE
In many pictures, Azhi Dahaka is shown with six eyes and three pairs of fangs on each terrifying head. In others, he has two piercing eyes and an array of gruesome teeth.

HEADS
Each of the heads is said to represent a different state of being or emotion: pain, anguish, and death.

TONGUE
Azhi Dahaka is said to have a long forked tongue, like a snake's, in each of his mouths.

TAIL
An enormous, slashing tail makes the monster even more of a weapon of mass destruction.

A cross between a dragon and a snake, the most striking thing about this giant monster is the three nightmarish heads rearing up from its scaly body. It is an ancient demon, created to bring havoc and destruction to the human world. Any adversary should be wary of its bite, which can inflict dreadful pain on anyone who is bitten. It attacks over and over again, each of its heads striking in a different direction.

Azhi Dahaka appears in the pre-Islamic religion of Zoroastrianism, where it is depicted as a huge dragon-serpent with thick, scaly armor and chaos in his eyes. In Persian mythology, the good god Ahura Mazda is permanently fighting the evil god, Ahriman. Azhi Dahaka is a destroying dragon created by Ahriman to eat the universe and put out the glorious light of the heavens. The dragon is hunted by Atar, son of the good god, who chains him to a mountain. It is said that he will break free of his shackles at the end of human time, starting the final battle between good and evil, in which one third of the human race will be destroyed in his anger.

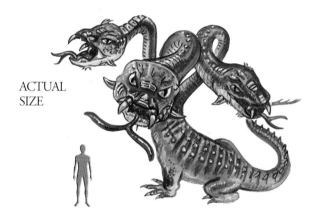

ACTUAL
SIZE

WHERE IN THE WORLD?

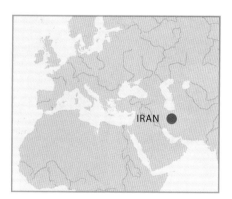

IRAN ●

These tales are part of a Persian religion from the 6th century BC. Persia is the old name for the country of Iran.

DID YOU KNOW?

• In some stories, his name is spelled differently: Azi Dahaka. In one myth, he is a storm demon who steals cattle and then begins to prey upon humans.

• Persian war banners often showed dragons, and the old Persian name for these creatures was *azdahag*. His name may also be a pun on the word *dah* meaning ten, having ten sins.

• Ahriman and Ahura Mazda are twin brothers. Ahura Mazda is the spirit of supreme good, god of light, and ruler of the universe. He is the creator of humans and makes his son Atar especially to fight the three-headed dragon.

• In the story, the eternal battle between good and evil will only end when Atar kills the dragon and scatters its ashes into the gulf of oblivion.

Camazotz

EARS
This bat-man's ears are huge, giving him the true supersonic hearing that a real bat uses to "see" in the dark.

WINGS
Camazotz has the wings of a bat but, unlike a true bat, he also has fingers and thumbs. The fingers of a true bat are the supporting bones that spread the wings and allow the bat to fly.

FACE
Many bats have this leaf-nosed face to help with their echolocation skills. Not so many have the wild eyes, and only vampire bats live on a diet of blood.

BODY
He has the body of a man and wears typical Mayan clothing and golden neck jewelry. Check his feet though: bat claws for toes!

Around 100 BC, the Zapotec Indians of Mexico worshipped an unusual bat-god known as Camazotz. He had the body of a man but the face, wings, and claws of a bat. Camazotz had the leaf nose, sharp teeth, and specialized tongue of the blood-drinking vampire bat. His followers offered bloody sacrifices to their god, who represented darkness and death.

ACTUAL SIZE

Camazotz lived deep in a cavern, hanging from the ceiling and emerging from his roost as the sun disappeared for the day. Like a vampire bat, he could fly silently, swooping his large, leathery wings, but he could also walk strongly and stealthily to creep up on his unsuspecting victims. The Mayan Hero twins called Hunahpu and Xbalanque had to undergo many trials in the underworld. One of these was to spend the night in the bat cavern, where they attempted to keep back the demon creature until dawn. Peeping from his hiding place, Hunahpu gets his head slashed off by Camazotz. His distraught brother called to all the other animals to bring him their favorite fruit. The coati brought a squash, which made a good substitute head, and the two brothers were able to defeat the bat god.

WHERE IN THE WORLD?

MEXICO AND GUATEMALA

The story of Hunahpu, Xbalanque, and Camazotz is told in the Popol Vuh, the creation story of the Mayans who lived in Mexico and Guatemala.

DID YOU KNOW?

• The book of the Popol Vuh describes Camazotz's cavern as "Zotzilaha: the house of bats." It was home to many bats that swooped and screeched around the heads of Hunahpu and Xbalanque during their terrifying night there.

• In Peru and Chile, the bat god is known as the *chonchon* and is the head of a dead person that has grown huge ears that flap and lift the head off its shoulders.

• Camazotz means "death bat" in the K'iche' language spoken by Mayans in Guatemala. The language is still spoken there as a second language (after Spanish).

• In some tales, Camazotz was turned to stone in the daytime and came to life again every night.

Cthulhu

HEAD
Cthulhu's head is a mass of tentacles, writhing around its lower jaw. It is soft and pulpy and covered with suckers, with a mouth full of rows and rows of terrifying teeth.

WINGS
This enormous beast has a pair of tiny wings, which are not large enough to allow it to fly, but add to its monstrous appearance.

CLAWS
The giant claws on its hands are large enough to pierce a man through the chest but are dwarfed by the huge claws of its hind feet.

BODY
The grotesque, rubbery body is covered in scales and looks bloated from its life beneath the ocean.

This horrifying creation is a character from fiction, invented by the horror writer H. P. Lovecraft in 1926. Cthulhu is the high priest of the Great Old Ones, an alien race who inhabited the Earth before humans came along. They lived in the huge stone city of R'Iyeh until it sank beneath the ocean. Cthulhu is now slumbering beneath the waves, waiting for the time when the island and its monstrous inhabitants will rise again.

In "The Call of Cthulhu," the city of R'Iyeh is briefly pushed back above the ocean surface by an earthquake. A Norwegian sailor named Gustaf Johansen lands on the island, and he and his shipmates explore the damp, slime-covered, eerie stone city in amazement. The sailors stupidly look behind a huge stone door, which releases Cthulhu. He kills all but two of the men, who manage to run back to their ship. They set sail, full steam ahead, and sail straight at the sea monster, breaking him apart—but not for long…

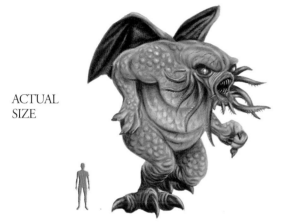

ACTUAL
SIZE

WHERE IN THE WORLD?

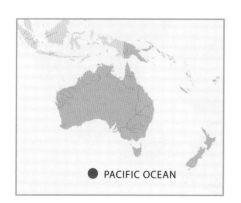

● PACIFIC OCEAN

Cthulhu lies "dead but dreaming" in the sunken city of R'Iyeh, hidden deep beneath the waves of the Pacific Ocean.

DID YOU KNOW?

• Cthulhu's name can be pronounced in different ways: "kloo-hloo" and "ka-thoo-loo" are both common. Even Lovecraft, the author, said it in different ways. He said that it was difficult for a human to make the alien sounds needed.

• The giant creature first appeared in the short story "The Call of Cthulhu" which was featured in a book called *Weird Tales* in 1928. Cthulhu also has been in some of Lovecraft's other stories.

• The Great Old Ones first came to Earth in an explosion of stars, from the planet Vhoorl. They are made up of alien matter.

• Cthulhu doesn't look particularly cuddly, but a range of plush toys has been made with a green Cthulhu, a black one, and even a Santa Cthulhu!

Cyclops

ARMS
Bulging with muscles, the long arms pound out metal and shift stone blocks with ease.

EYE
One huge, watchful eye stares from the center of the cyclops's forehead.

HAIR
Dirty, matted hair infested with lice sprouts wildy from the cyclops's head.

TEETH
When the cyclops wants a snack, he rips up humans with his big, pointed teeth.

CLAWS
Instead of nails, hooked claws grow from the fingers and toes. If the cyclops is in a bad mood, these make formidable weapons.

FEET
The whole ground shakes when the cyclops stamps around on his massive feet.

The single eye of the cyclops stares menacingly from its horrible, hairy face. This cruel, watchful giant can smash a human to pieces with a single flick of the wrist. In Greek mythology, the first cyclopes were three brothers called Steropes, Brontes, and Arges, sons of Ge (Mother Earth) and the god Uranus. They were blacksmiths by trade. The last race of cyclopes were brutish shepherds who lived squalid lives in dingy caves in Sicily, tending their flocks and tearing intruders apart. They communicated with grunts and roars. The cyclops Polyphemus was the most dreadful of all. When Odysseus and his men turned up at his cave, Polyphemus imprisoned them. Dashing out the brains of two men a day, he ate the men whole.

Odysseus waited patiently for the cyclops to fall asleep. Then the hero sharpened a stake and heated it in the fire. Driving the weapon into the scary giant's eye, Odysseus twisted the stake around, blinding Polyphemus. The survivors escaped the next day, clinging to the bellies of the cyclops's sheep as he sent them out to graze.

WHERE IN THE WORLD?

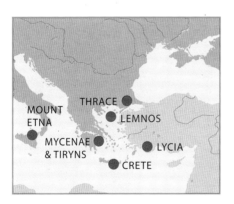

Cyclopes lived in the regions of Thrace in northeast Greece, in Lycia in southwest Turkey, and on the island of Crete. They worked in Hephaestus's forge on Lemnos, and built the cities of Mycenae and Tiryns. Later tales place them on Mount Etna in Sicily.

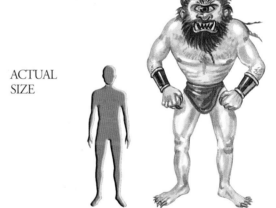

ACTUAL SIZE

DID YOU KNOW?

• The word "cyclops" comes from the Greek words *kyklos* ("circle") and *ops* ("eye"). The names of the cyclopes, Brontes, Steropes, and Arges, meant "thunder," "lightning bolt," and "lightning flash."

• The cyclops myth may have its origins in an ancient guild of Greek metal workers in Thrace, who had circles tattooed on their foreheads.

• Some people believe that the legend of the cyclopes arose when the ancient Greeks first encountered elephants.

FEROCIOUS GIANTS

Fomorian

EYE
The Fomorian Balor's eye was huge. Its piercing gaze killed anyone who saw him.

MISSHAPEN
Some Formorians were missing arms or legs, while others had multiple limbs.

SIZE
In many tales, the Fomorians are a race of giants, capable of pitching stones as big as a human with just one enormous hand.

SKIN
The skin was green, slimy, and oozed drops of poisonous sweat.

FORM
With a vile mix of animal and human body parts, the Fomorians were repulsive to look at.

The Fomorians were an ancient race who, in Celtic folklore, were the first people of Ireland. Ireland was invaded by the Firbolgs, who transformed the Fomorians into gruesome giant monsters with the body of a man and the head of an animal. They preyed upon the farms around them, demanding food, and if their demands were not met, they took human replacements. Anyone who tried to stand up to them was punished by having their nose sliced off their face.

 In the Irish Mythological Cycle tales, the Fomorians are a race of sea gods who marry and join forces with the Tuatha Dé Danann tribe of gods. Lug Lámfhota, the grandson of a purebred Fomorian, enters a battle against the Fomorian known as Balor of the Evil Eye. In the end, Lug wins by pitching a stone from his slingshot that pushes Balor's eye back through his head and into the heart of the Fomorian army. This brings the downfall of the whole Fomorian race in Ireland, and they are forced back into the sea.

ACTUAL SIZE

WHERE IN THE WORLD?

ATLANTIC OCEAN

IRELAND

The Fomorians were said to have emerged from the north Atlantic and settled along Ireland's rugged west coast.

DID YOU KNOW?

• The Irish name for the Fomorians was "Fomhóire," which means "beneath the sea." They were the first race to come to Ireland, but didn't invade inland areas.

• In later folklore, the Fomorians were linked to the natural elements, described as weather spirits that could blight crops and bring storms and fog.

• A curse cast while standing on one leg, with one eye closed, and one arm behind your back, is supposed to have greater magical power.

• The Irish poet W. B. Yeats (1865–1939) wrote about the Fomorians, spelling their name "Fomor" or "Fomoroh."

• The name "Fomorians" is sometimes used for any band of pirates or sea raiders, especially ones who settle in one place.

Frankenstein's Monster

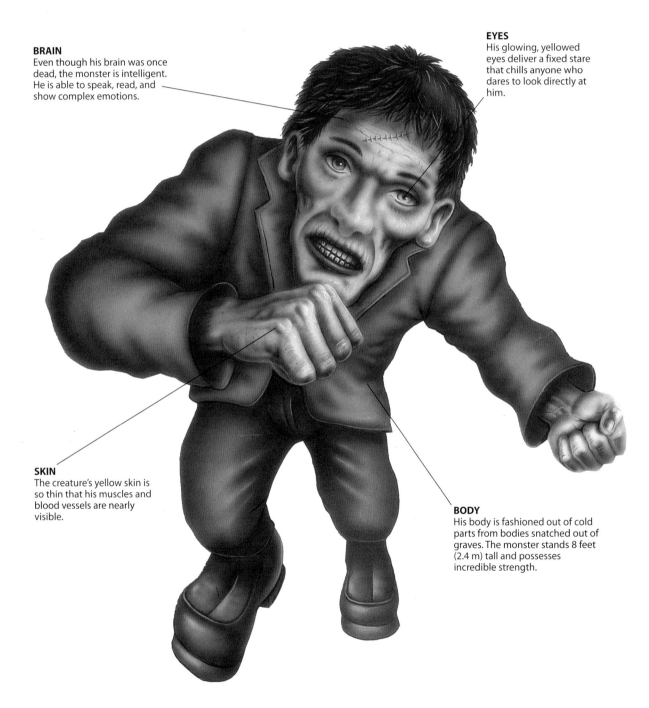

BRAIN
Even though his brain was once dead, the monster is intelligent. He is able to speak, read, and show complex emotions.

EYES
His glowing, yellowed eyes deliver a fixed stare that chills anyone who dares to look directly at him.

SKIN
The creature's yellow skin is so thin that his muscles and blood vessels are nearly visible.

BODY
His body is fashioned out of cold parts from bodies snatched out of graves. The monster stands 8 feet (2.4 m) tall and possesses incredible strength.

Pieced together from body parts stolen from graves, Frankenstein's monster is a terrible reminder that man should not attempt to play God. Victor Frankenstein believes that electricity can be used as a power source to bring the dead back to life. He harnesses powers meant only for God, and the result is that he creates a monster that destroys him.

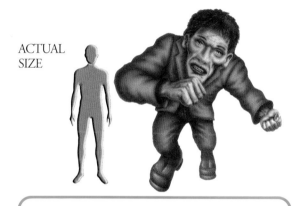

ACTUAL
SIZE

Frankenstein conducts a series of experiments on stolen corpses. When a bolt of lightning brings his monster to life in the lab, Frankenstein is immediately sorry. He intended his creation to be beautiful, but it is revolting. Horrified, Frankenstein runs away from his awful creation. Frankenstein awakes to see the ghastly monster standing at his bedside. Once again, he flees his creation. When Frankenstein's brother is murdered, the monster admits killing him as a way to strike back at his creator for rejecting him. The lonely monster begs Frankenstein to create a mate for him. Frankenstein begins work on a female creature, but his conscience forces him to destroy her and dump her lifeless body in a lake. As revenge, the furious monster murders Frankenstein's bride on their wedding night.

WHERE IN THE WORLD?

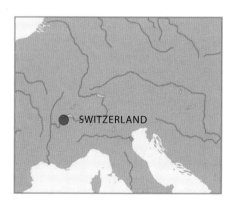

SWITZERLAND

The secret lab where Victor Frankenstein brings his monster to life is in an unknown location near Geneva, Switzerland.

DID YOU KNOW?

• **Frankenstein spends the rest of his life pursuing the monster to take revenge for the death of his bride. He tracks the creature to the icy Arctic and chases him on a dogsled, but the ice between them separates in a huge crack. When Frankenstein dies, the monster weeps over the body of his creator. The creature heads off across the ice to die alone.**

• **Mary Shelley wrote the novel *Frankenstein* when she was 19 years old.**

• **The name "Frankenstein" is often incorrectly used to refer to Victor Frankenstein's creation. Throughout the book, his creation is referred to as "the creature" or "the monster." Frankenstein is the name of the scientist who created the monster.**

Gargantua

HEAD
Even before the age of two, his head was so big that each of his hats needed nearly 4,843 sq feet (450 sq m) of fabric.

BELLY
Fat Gargantua was so heavy, he needed a horse the size of six elephants to carry him about.

HANDS
His pudgy fists could hold herds of cattle. The gloves he wore on cold days were made from the skins of 16 hobgoblins and trimmed with three werewolf pelts.

LEGS & FEET
Gargantua's stockings took more than 5,381 sq feet (500 sq m) of wool. The soles of his shoes were the stitched hides of 1,100 brown cows.

This giant of legend was known for his huge appetite and crushing size. He once uprooted a mighty tree and used it to flatten the castle of his archenemy, King Picrochole. The defenders tried to kill him, but he thought their cannonballs were just buzzing flies. Later, at home, he combed the cannonballs from his hair using a comb 984 feet (300 m) long with teeth of elephant's tusks.

ACTUAL
SIZE

Six pilgrims find themselves without a roof over their heads at dusk. So, they shelter in the vegetable garden of a great castle, hiding in some straw among giant cabbages and lettuces. The castle is the home of Grandgousier, Gargantua's father. Feeling hungry, Gargantua grabs several lettuces in one hand, and with them five of the terrified pilgrims. He almost drowns them by seasoning them with oil and vinegar, then crams them into his mouth with the lettuces. The last pilgrim has hidden beneath a lettuce—but his staff sticks out, and Gargantua, believing it to be a snail's eyestalk, stuffs him into his mouth, too. Then one of the pilgrims, tapping with his staff before him, hits the nerve of a rotten tooth. Bawling in pain, Gargantua sends for a toothpick and loosens the pilgrims, who flee for their lives.

WHERE IN THE WORLD?

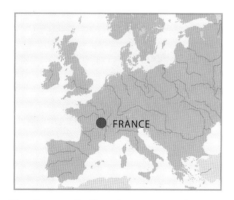

FRANCE

The legend of a giant named Gargantua may have come from Celtic tribes in northern France centuries before Rabelais wrote his book. Rabelais was born in Chinon, a town to the southwest of Paris. It was here that he set many of Gargantua's adventures.

DID YOU KNOW?

• To this day, the word "gargantuan" means "huge," and it is often used to describe a massive appetite.

• The 16th-century writer François Rabelais used his version of Gargantua to poke fun at the powerful, vain, and pompous people in French society.

• Rabelais wrote that Gargantua fathered a son, Pantagruel, when he was 524 years old!

Gogmagog

STATURE
Gogmagog stood almost 13 feet (4 m) tall and was so strong he could rip up trees by the roots.

HEAD
Wild haired, slack mouthed and piggy eyed, Gogmagog was incredibly ugly by human standards.

BODY
Clothed in roughly stitched animal skins, the giant's body bulged with muscle.

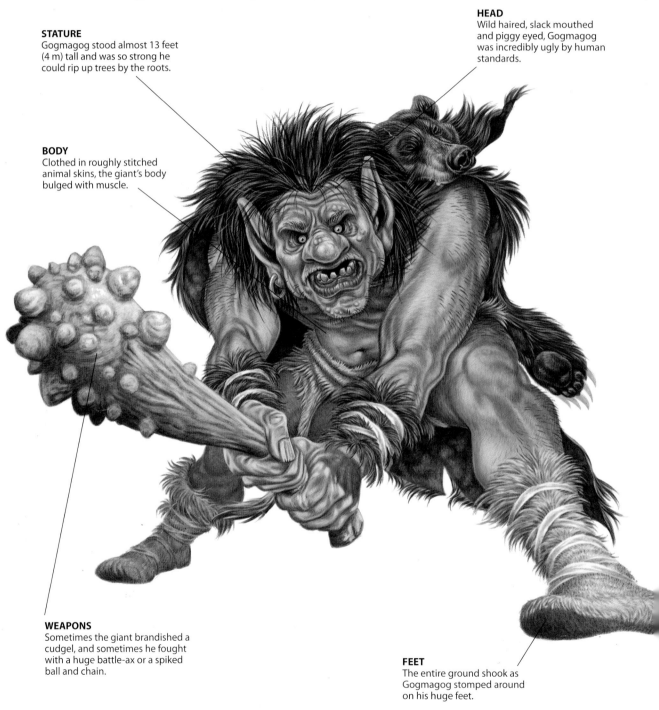

WEAPONS
Sometimes the giant brandished a cudgel, and sometimes he fought with a huge battle-ax or a spiked ball and chain.

FEET
The entire ground shook as Gogmagog stomped around on his huge feet.

ogmagog was one of the last of the mighty giants of Albion, a demonic race of fiercely aggressive beings who lived on the island that later became Britain. The giants were spawned by one of the exiled daughters of the Roman emperor Diocletian and a demon. Despite their great power, they were soon threatened by a Trojan invasion. The giants vigorously resisted the Trojan soldiers and initially drove them back, but their army was defeated after the invaders dug hidden trenches full of stakes. The giants succumbed to the Trojans' superior fighting skills until, finally, only Gogmagog was left alive. He, too, was finally killed by the Trojan warrior Corineus.

 Only 20 giants escaped the Trojans' deadly traps, including Gogmagog, the strongest of them all. He waited until the invaders were celebrating a day dedicated to the gods, then led the others in a frenzied attack. The rampaging giants tore many Trojans limb from limb, while Gogmagog simply picked them up and killed them in one blow. But Brutus and Corineus rallied their men and, one by one, the giants were overwhelmed.

WHERE IN THE WORLD?

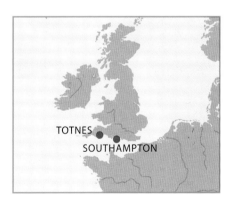

TOTNES
SOUTHAMPTON

According to legend, the Trojans landed in Albion (Britain) at the site of either modern Totnes or modern Southampton. Gogmagog met his fate in the sea close to Totnes, where a cliff still bears the name Lan-Goenagog, or Giant's Leap.

ACTUAL
SIZE

DID YOU KNOW?

• In legend, the warrior Brutus renamed Albion "Britain" after himself, and after receiving the west of the country as his share, the warrior Corineus called it "Cornwall."

• Many associate the names Gog and Magog with the hostile forces of Satan, which are due to appear just before the end of the world.

• Tales of giants may have been inspired by huge prehistoric figures cut into the chalk hills of Britain.

Golem

MUSCLES
If allowed, a golem can grow immensely strong. When it is on one of its rampages, it can hurl boulders around as if they were pebbles.

FOREHEAD
One way to bring a golem to life is to write a special word on its forehead. Erasing the word is then the only way to kill the monster.

MOUTH
While most golems can't talk, a few have supposedly had limited powers of speech.

HANDS
These grow bigger and stronger all the time and are a rampant golem's main tools of destruction.

SKIN
A golem is usually made of clay, stone, or wood, so its "skin" is hard and rough to the touch, and extremely tough.

FACE
A golem often looks like its creator and master. When obedient, the creature is expressionless—but if it grows too big, it can fly into a terrifying rage.

FEET
A golem run wild can kick down solid doors with ease.

A golem is one of mythology's more unusual creatures. It is a figure made from clay, wood, or stone and then brought to life by its creator. Once living, the golem then acts as a guardian and protector over its creator, and it obeys its master's every command. Ominously, the golem also grows bigger and stronger every day. Here is the danger. If the golem becomes too large, it can become wild and destructive. The creator must destroy and rebuild it before it becomes out of control and a danger to everyone.

An absent-minded golem maker neglected to destroy his creation, and the beast grew so huge and monstrous that it ransacked its master's house. The devastation may not end there, though, for if no one can reach up to erase the magical, life-giving word from the creature's forehead, it may end up obliterating everything—and everybody—in its path.

WHERE IN THE WORLD?

EASTERN EUROPE

Historically, golems have most often been made in eastern Europe, but a golem can be created from such a range of widely abundant and easily available materials that a sorcerer can make one almost anywhere in the world, at any time.

ACTUAL SIZE

DID YOU KNOW?

• Tibetans have their own golem, a tulpa, which obeys orders but can develop a personality of its own.

• Vietnamese sorcerers called the Thay Phap make human puppets out of wood or straw, breathe life into them, and order them to rob and kill.

• In Spain in the 11th century, the philosopher Solomon ibn Gabirol was acquitted of sorcery after he agreed to destroy his female golem.

Grendel

HEAD
The oversized head is so heavy that when Beowulf cuts it off, four men are required to carry it away.

MOUTH
Grendel's powerful jaw is lined with sharp, unbreakable teeth that are perfect for crunching through the bones of his enemies.

EYES
A horrible light like a fire in his eyes reflects the hatred he feels toward all human beings.

SKIN
Grendel's skin cannot be broken. He has placed a charm on all human weapons so that they cannot harm him.

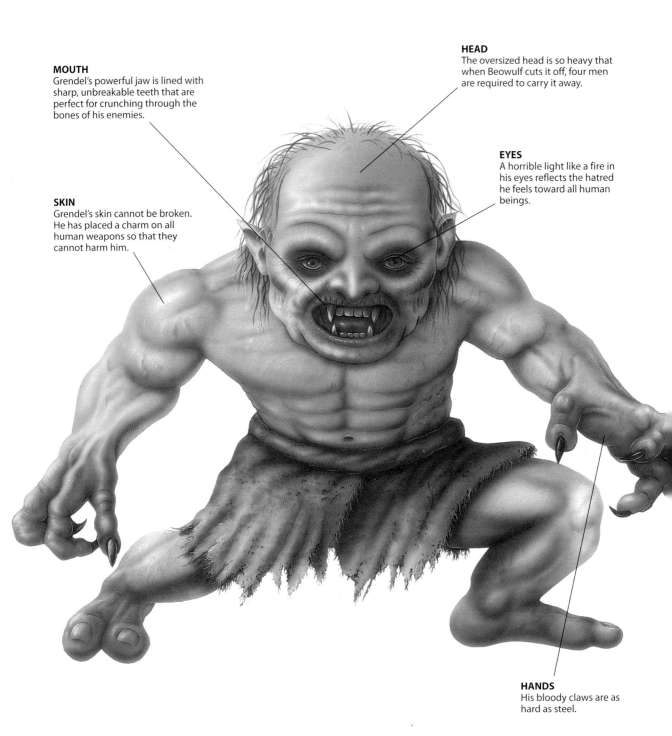

HANDS
His bloody claws are as hard as steel.

As an outcast in the epic poem *Beowulf*, Grendel walks in desolate places on the fringes of society. Angered by the sounds of singing and celebration coming from the feasting hall, Grendel wages war for 12 years against the Danes. A furious and hungry creature, he leaves behind scenes of carnage and bloody footprints. Killing more than 30 warriors in the feasting hall, he drags away their bodies to eat them in his swamp lair.

Grendel cannot be stopped. He has placed a magical charm on all human weapons, which means that no knife, arrow, spear, or sword can harm him. The king and his people abandon the feasting hall. Only the hero Beowulf is unafraid. Beowulf and his men spend the night in the feasting hall. As they sleep, Grendel enters and attacks, devouring one of Beowulf's soldiers. Beowulf is only pretending to sleep. He leaps up and grasps Grendel's hand in a death grip. Beowulf's men come to his aid, but their weapons cannot pierce Grendel's skin. Beowulf summons all his strength and, using only his bare hands, rips Grendel's arm off. Grendel retreats to his swamp to die, leaving a trail of blood behind him.

ACTUAL SIZE

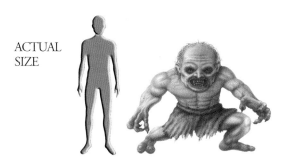

WHERE IN THE WORLD?

GEATLAND

The outcast Grendel and his man-eating habits are known throughout Geatland, a region in the south of Sweden.

DID YOU KNOW?

• Grendel dies in his cave beneath the swamp. Grendel's mother, who is also a terrible beast, attacks the feasting hall, seeking revenge for the death of her son. Beowulf tracks her to the swamp cave, where she battles Beowulf and comes close to defeating the great hero. Fortunately, Beowulf notices a sword and uses it to kill Grendel's mother.

• Beowulf finds Grendel's corpse in the cave, removes the head with the sword, and keeps it as a battle trophy, proving his victory over the dreadful menace. The king rewards Beowulf for ridding Geatland of Grendel and his gruesome mother.

• Grendel is a descendant of Cain, the first murderer in the Bible.

Kronos

SICKLE
This is the weapon Kronos used to castrate his father, and also a sign of the harvest that he represents. A sickle is used to cut down grain in the fields.

CROW
This bird is a mistaken identity for Kronos, whose name may come from the word "korone" which means "crow" in Greek.

AGE
The gods live much longer than mortal beings. When Kronos was hundreds of years old, Zeus released him from his prison and made him king of the Elysian Fields (home of the blessed dead).

BLOOD
In some tales, the blood of Kronos's father splashes on the Earth and produces more children, such as the Furies (three sisters with a bad attitude).

Kronos was the offspring of Gaia and Uranus. He was the youngest of the Titans but was enraged by his father's cruelty to his family. Encouraged by his mother, he took a sickle and castrated his father, and took his place as ruler. He and his wife, Rhea, ruled together and gave birth to a new generation of gods. He was warned in a prophecy that his own children would rise against him, and so he took drastic measures. Each time a child was born, he ate it, to keep it safe and whole inside him where it could do him no harm.

ACTUAL
SIZE

Understandably, Rhea was not happy that all of her children were being devoured. She hid her last born, Zeus, in a cave, and tricked Kronos into eating a rock instead, wrapped in baby clothes. Zeus grew up in the cave, raised by the divine goat Amaltheia. When Zeus was old enough, he forced Kronos to regurgitate the children he had eaten, and then led them into battle against him. Kronos was sent into exile, either in Tartarus or Italy, where he ruled as Saturn according to some tales.

WHERE IN THE WORLD?

The cave on Mount Dicte, where Zeus was said to be raised, is a tourist site on Crete even today.

DID YOU KNOW?

• Gaia and Uranus had 12 Titan children, including Kronos and Rhea. The Titans are less famous in mythology than their offspring (or nieces and nephews), the Olympian gods, such as Zeus.

• In ancient Athens, a festival called Kronia was held on the twelfth day of the month of Hekatombaion (the first month of the Athenean calendar) to celebrate the harvest.

• Kronos and Rhea ruled during the Golden Age, a time of peace and well-being. After the Golden Age come the Silver, Bronze, and Iron Ages, and then the current time, which is seen as a bad time when things are getting worse than ever before.

• Zeus had five brothers and sisters, each swallowed by their father: Demeter, Hestia, Hera, Hades, and Poseidon.

Leviathan

FINS
Spiny pectoral fins easily slice flesh from bone but also come in handy when the monster wants to drag his massive body onto rocks.

SCALES
Tougher than the stoutest shield and tightly overlapping, these form an impenetrable armor that makes the monster invulnerable to human weapons such as swords, spears, and harpoons.

JAWS
No one escapes the gaping jaws, which are lined with rows of terrible teeth and belch out sparks and flames.

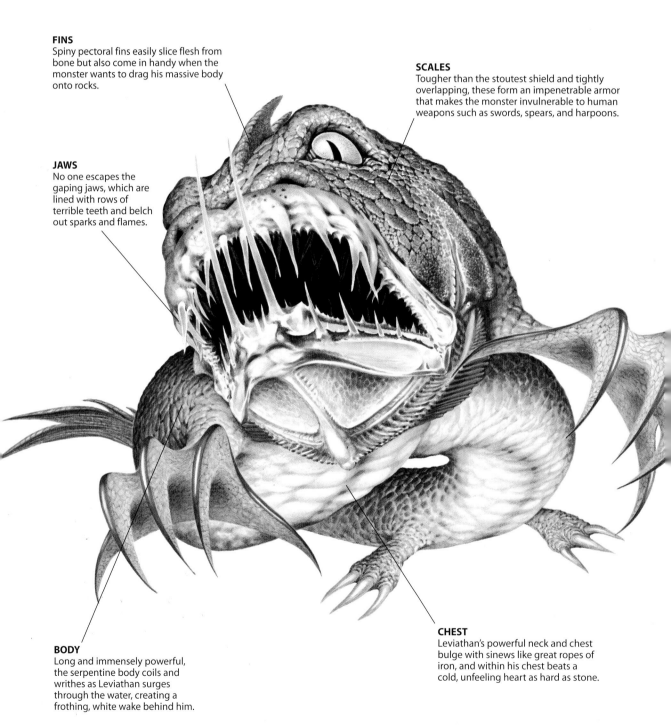

BODY
Long and immensely powerful, the serpentine body coils and writhes as Leviathan surges through the water, creating a frothing, white wake behind him.

CHEST
Leviathan's powerful neck and chest bulge with sinews like great ropes of iron, and within his chest beats a cold, unfeeling heart as hard as stone.

This primeval sea monster dominates the watery wastes of the world and has power over all the creatures of the ocean. He is chaos and evil personified, and he brings death and disaster in his foaming wake. His body stinks like a rotten carcass and he drinks the entire flow of rivers every day. His furnace-hot breath makes the sea boil, and when he sneezes, smoke billows from his nose. The Leviathan is first mentioned in Middle Eastern creation myths dating back more than 5,000 years ago. According to Hebrew texts, Yahweh (God) made Leviathan and a female mate on the fifth day of creation but promptly killed the female to stop her producing offspring that might destabilize the world.

Stirring up the ocean with his mighty tail, Leviathan created a seething wall of water that gathered speed, burst over the shore and completely overwhelmed a small fishing village. Huts were shattered like matchwood and screaming victims were swept out to their deaths. A few locals escaped the carnage by climbing trees, and they could only watch in horror as the monster reared out of the water to gloat at his handiwork and gobble up anyone washed out to sea.

WHERE IN THE WORLD?

Leviathan has his origins in early Hebrew writings from the Middle East, dating back to about 3000 BC. The Hebrews occupied Turkey, Syria, Jordan, Israel, Iraq, and Iran—but the monster has the run of all the world's oceans.

ACTUAL SIZE

DID YOU KNOW?

• Early images of Leviathan from seal stones and weapons show the monster with seven heads.

• Christians have identified Leviathan with Satan, with his huge mouth being the entrance to hell.

• Most fish swim willingly into Leviathan's jaws, apart from the tiny stickleback. This he fears—for the stickleback was created to keep him in check.

Mongolian Death Worm

SIZE
It is around two feet (0.6 m) long and as thick as a man's arm. It may have a thinner tail end, but some reports say it is blunt and untapered, as if it has been cut off.

COLOR
Not the usual pale pink of an earthworm, the death worm is said to be bright red, like blood or salami.

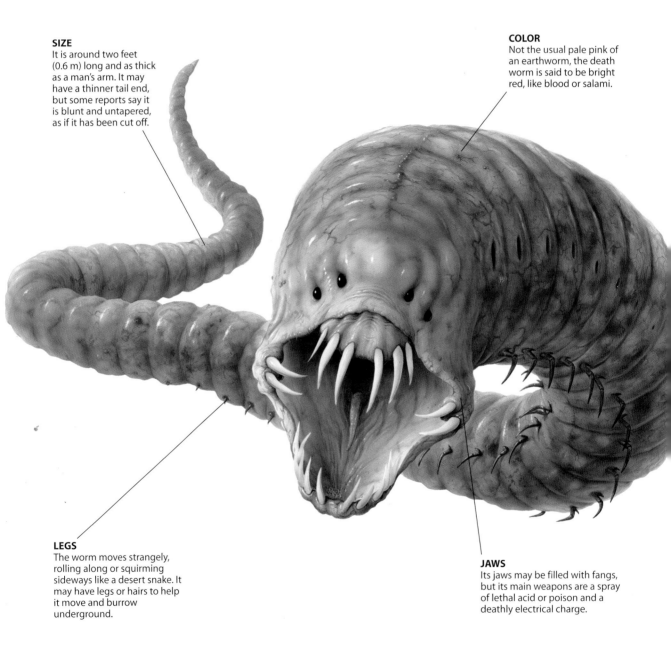

LEGS
The worm moves strangely, rolling along or squirming sideways like a desert snake. It may have legs or hairs to help it move and burrow underground.

JAWS
Its jaws may be filled with fangs, but its main weapons are a spray of lethal acid or poison and a deathly electrical charge.

The Mongolian death worm is also known as the "intestine worm" because of its resemblance to the large intestines of a cow. No one truly knows how it feeds and kills. Some say it can squirt venom or acid, some say that it gives off an electrical charge that can kill from a distance. It hibernates for ten months of the year and comes out in the hottest months, June and July. It's said, though, that it mostly appears after rain, when the ground is wet.

Does this creature hunt and kill for fun, or just for food? No one knows for sure. Many tales are told of nomads roaming the solitary wastelands where the worm has been seen, and never returning to their family. The worm is able to strike down a horse with a charge of electricity, leaving the rider alone and far from any human help. Without a horse to escape, the nomad has to face his fate: a shot of the worm's lethal death juice, right in the eyes.

ACTUAL SIZE

WHERE IN THE WORLD?

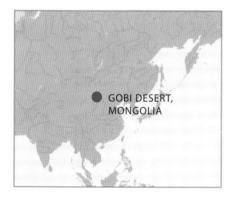

GOBI DESERT, MONGOLIA

The death worm sightings are all in the dry, rocky, inhospitable Gobi Desert, one of the world's largest deserts.

DID YOU KNOW?

• The worm is attracted to the color yellow, and one story tells how he found a yellow toy box and killed the child who opened it.

• Early written reports of the death worm come from the book *On the Trail of Ancient Men* by Professor Roy Chapman Andrews, said to be the inspiration for the character of Indiana Jones. He was not convinced of the existence of the worm.

• There are many reports of sightings, including one by a Mongolian leader. There may be many more unreported sightings by people who did not live to tell the tale.

• A 2005 expedition by British scientists went in search of the worm. They did not find it, but agreed that people they met really believed in the worm. They did find two new species of lizard and snake, though.

FEROCIOUS GIANTS

Roc

HUGE WINGS
According to the explorer Marco Polo, the roc has a wingspan of 48 feet (15 m) and feathers 24 feet (7 m) long.

FABULOUS PLUMAGE
In some stories, the roc is described as being bright white all over, just like its eggs.

EVIL EYES
Each bigger than a person's head, these can spot a victim from far away—when not keeping watch over its enormous eggs.

VICIOUS CLAWS
The roc can pluck a 5-ton elephant from the ground with one claw, while a single slash from a talon can rip its belly wide open.

SNARLING MOUTH
Hooked and pointed, the great bill is full of dagger-like teeth. The tongue is forked like a snake's, and laps up the last drops of a victim's blood.

ROC

Imagine a bird of prey the size of a large aircraft, with talons as big as sabers and a huge bill full of jagged teeth. The ancient Persians did, and called it the roc. It is a mythical beast of enormous size and strength. When it appears overhead, day turns to night, thunder roars, and lightning flashes. The beat of its wings causes terrible winds to sweep across the land and sea, sinking ships and devastating all in its path. The roc nests in a fabulous jewel-filled valley, where it lays gigantic, glowing white eggs.

ACTUAL SIZE

Steering around the shores of Madagascar one day, sailors could barely believe their eyes when a monstrous bird flew overhead—carrying an elephant in its claws! Horrified, they watched it fly inland. As the sailors excitedly debated what they saw, the roc arrived on its nest to the accompaniment of squawks from its waiting chicks. The great bird ripped the elephant apart and fed it to its brood. But their hunger was not satisfied, and the roc was soon back in the air—and heading straight for the ship.

DID YOU KNOW?

• The roc—or "rukh" in Arabic—is thought to have inspired the rook in chess, a game which reached Europe from Persia in the 13th century.

• In one story in the famous book *The Arabian Nights Entertainments*, Sinbad the Sailor's men anger a pair of rocs by breaking one of their eggs. The rocs retaliate by pelting them with rocks, sinking one of their ships.

• According to legend, merchants collected jewels from the valley of the roc by pushing huge joints of mutton off the surrounding hilltops. As the meat rolled into the valley, it became studded with jewels. Rocs then swooped on the mutton—but before they could take it to the nest, the merchants would harass them into dropping it at their feet.

• The roc was reputed to be so strong that it could carry off a rhinoceros and an elephant at the same time.

WHERE IN THE WORLD?

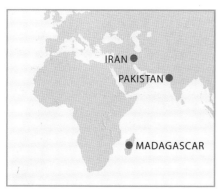

Stories about the roc originated in ancient Persia, which is now Iran. According to the oldest tales, it only ever landed on Mount Qaf, in modern Pakistan. In most stories, however, it is said to come from Madagascar, the large island off the eastern coast of Africa.

Shelob

LEGS
The ultrasensitive hairs on her legs detect movement and the scent of her prey approaching.

SKIN
Her bumpy, pitted hide is so thick that no weapon can pierce it.

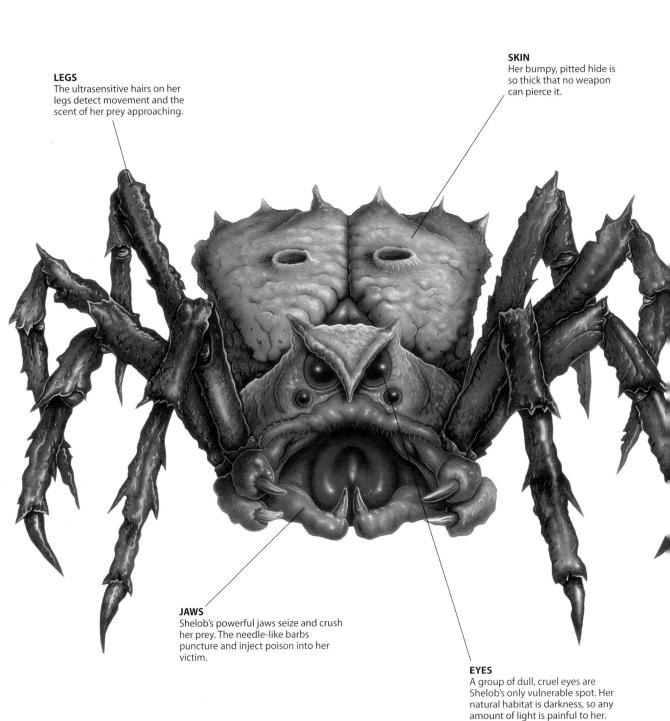

JAWS
Shelob's powerful jaws seize and crush her prey. The needle-like barbs puncture and inject poison into her victim.

EYES
A group of dull, cruel eyes are Shelob's only vulnerable spot. Her natural habitat is darkness, so any amount of light is painful to her.

A demon in spider form from J.R.R. Tolkien's *Lord of the Rings* books, Shelob lives in a dark, foul-smelling lair, and devours any living thing that approaches along Spider's Pass. The evil Lord Sauron uses Shelob to guard one of the entrances to his realm. Sauron throws her an Orc every few days to keep her happy. She spins ropelike webs that even a sword cannot break. She waits, the sensitive hairs on her legs detecting the approach of her next meal. When a victim is tangled in her web, she uses her stinger and needlelike jaws to pump a paralyzing poison into his veins.

Shelob is fat from drinking the blood of men, Orcs, and Elves. She finds a hobbit called Frodo in her lair and attacks him. Shelob stings Frodo in the neck, leaving him paralyzed and helpless. Frodo's friend Sam rips off one of Shelob's legs and puts out one of her eyes, which are the only soft spots on her body. In a fury, she tries to crush Sam beneath her massive body, but she is impaled on Frodo's sword. The injury is not enough to kill her, but she scurries away, wounded.

ACTUAL SIZE

WHERE IN THE WORLD?

MIDDLE-EARTH

MORDOR

Shelob awaits her next victim in the dark caverns located high in Middle-earth's mountains of Mordor, according to J.R.R. Tolkien's *The Two Towers*.

DID YOU KNOW?

• Frodo attempts to slash Shelob with his sword before she is able to attack him, but her armored skin cannot be cut open.

• Frodo lights the way through Shelob's lair using the Star-glass, which contains a fragment of the Evening Star's light. Shelob is accustomed to complete darkness, so the light from the Star-glass is painful to her eyes.

• Frodo and Sam are led into Spider's Pass by Gollum, a servant of Sauron. Gollum intends to steal the One Ring of Power from Frodo after Shelob devours Frodo and Sam.

• Shelob's webs are as strong as steel. She wraps her paralyzed victims in the silk she spins, and leaves them until she is ready to dine on their blood.

Talos

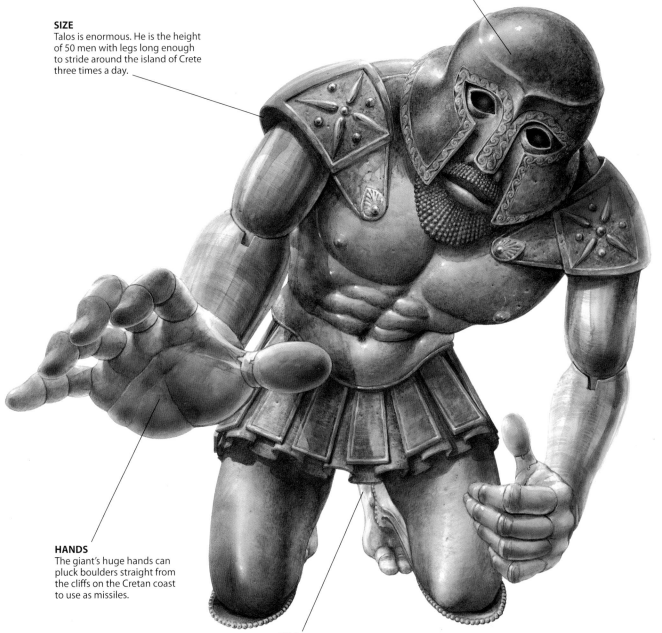

HELMET
Talos's armor and helmet make him look menacing, but he doesn't really need them for protection as his whole body is made of metal.

SIZE
Talos is enormous. He is the height of 50 men with legs long enough to stride around the island of Crete three times a day.

HANDS
The giant's huge hands can pluck boulders straight from the cliffs on the Cretan coast to use as missiles.

HEEL
His weak spot is his heel, where the giant vein that runs from the top to bottom of his body is plugged by a single bronze pin.

This giant from Greek and Roman myths is actually a walking, living statue made from bronze. His purpose is to patrol the island of Crete three times a day to keep watch for invaders and pirates. When spotted, he pounds them with rocks or grabs them and clutches them to his chest. Then he leaps into the flames of a fire until his body becomes so hot that his prisoners burn to death. His weakness is the pin at the bottom of the vein that carries his ichor, or molten lead lifeblood, around his body.

Jason and his Argonauts were sailing back from their adventures in Colchis near the Black Sea. They needed to stop for fresh water and sailed to Crete to ask Talos's permission to come ashore. Talos refused, and Jason's wife, Medea, used her witchcraft to defeat him. As the metal giant gazed at her, he slumped onto the rocks and could not get up. She drew the pin from his heel and let the blood flow out until he was dead and no longer a threat.

ACTUAL SIZE

WHERE IN THE WORLD?

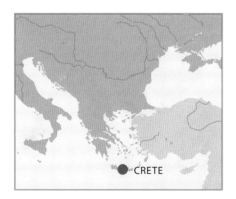

CRETE

Talos kept watch over the Greek island of Crete. He was a present from Zeus to the King of Crete, Minos.

DID YOU KNOW?

• The phrase "sardonic grin," which means a sneering or mocking smile, comes from a story about Talos. When he captured invaders from Sardinia and leapt into the fire, he had a wild grimace on his face.

• In some versions of the story, Talos dies in different ways. Sometimes he scrapes his delicate heel on the craggy rocks. Sometimes one of the Argonauts, Poias, shoots a poisoned arrow into his heel.

• Pictures of the giant with wings on his back are to symbolize how speedy he was traveling around the island three times a day.

• Talos has been featured as a character or a name in *Doctor Who, X-Men: The Animated Series, Stargate Atlantis, Star Trek, Babylon 5,* and the film *Jason and the Argonauts* (as well as other movies and TV series).

Thunderbird

EYES
Each time the thunderbird opens its eyes, bolts of lightning flash from the sky.

BACK
The thunderbird can carry an entire lake of water on its mighty back, releasing the water in torrential downpours.

WINGS
Powerful wings with feathers as long as canoe paddles send claps of thunder echoing through the air.

FEET
Huge, curved talons tip each toe, like those of a giant eagle or vulture.

HEADS
A second head sprouts from the thunderbird's chest, and both heads are equipped with viciously hooked beaks.

THUNDERBIRD

This gigantic, two-headed bird of prey is known by Native American tribes to bring thunder and lightning to the skies. Lightning bolts shoot from its eyes, storm clouds are carried on its wings, and an entire lake of water on its back makes torrential downpours. Some tribes believe that the thunderbird is the great creator spirit that made the heavens and the earth.

ACTUAL SIZE

◄——— 3 MILES (5 KM) ———►

WHERE IN THE WORLD?

NORTH AMERICA ●

Thunderbirds are part of the belief systems held by many groups of Native Americans, from the Inuit peoples in the Arctic, to the Aztecs in Mexico. These gigantic birds are thought to live either in the sky or in remote mountain caves.

The Nootka people of Vancouver Island, off British Columbia, called the thunderbird Tootooch. To them, it was the sole survivor of four giant birds that preyed on whales. By turning into a whale, the god Quawteaht tricked the birds into attacking him. He lured three to their death as he dived deep, but the survivor flew to the heavens. The story probably reflects the fact that storms often come from just one point on the compass. In the tales of the Quillayute people of the Olympic Peninsula in Washington State, the thunderbird and killer whale are deadly enemies. They once fought a fierce battle, shaking the mountains and uprooting trees as they struggled, creating vast treeless plains. Every time the thunderbird seized the whale in its talons, the whale managed to escape, finally retreating into the deep ocean.

DID YOU KNOW?

• **Many Native American tribes claim to have seen the thunderbird, and in South Dakota they believe it has left huge footprints. The prints are 25 miles (40 km) apart in an area known as Thunder Tracks, near the source of the Minnesota River.**

• **Some stories say that the thunderbird lives in a mountain cave, burying its food in a dark hole in the ice. If hunters come too close, it rolls huge lumps of ice down the mountainside to scare them away.**

Troll

FACE
Trolls are famous for being ugly—period. The only pretty trolls are the females in Norway, which are said to be beautiful with long, red hair.

BRAINS
A troll's head is small and its brain is even smaller. It eats first and thinks later (if it thinks at all).

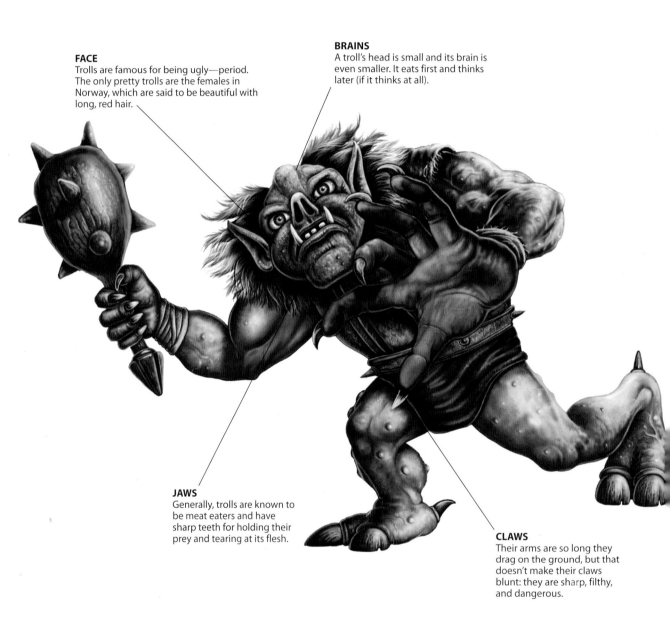

JAWS
Generally, trolls are known to be meat eaters and have sharp teeth for holding their prey and tearing at its flesh.

CLAWS
Their arms are so long they drag on the ground, but that doesn't make their claws blunt: they are sharp, filthy, and dangerous.

In the earliest accounts, trolls are giant creatures who only come out at night. If they are caught in the daylight, they turn to stone. Trolls are also infamous for being ugly, violent, greedy, mean-spirited, and dim-witted, but ultimately dangerous. That's not a good combination for a creature that is stronger than a wrestling champ with muscles like a bodybuilder. That's why many Scandinavians still avoid lonely woods and hills after dark.

The most famous tale of a troll is the Three Billy Goats Gruff. Three goats have eaten all the grass on their side of the river. To get food on the other side, they have to pass the troll who lives under the bridge. The littlest goat crosses first, and persuades the greedy troll not to eat him as he is not fat enough. The medium-sized goat does the same. When the biggest goat crosses, he is strong enough to throw the troll into the stream with his horns, and the bridge is safe to cross for all time.

ACTUAL SIZE

WHERE IN THE WORLD?

SCANDINAVIA

Trolls feature heavily in the fairy tales of Scandinavian countries, where they are also called "Trold" or "Trolld."

DID YOU KNOW?

• Trolls live underground in large communities. Their homes are palaces, stuffed full of treasure that sometimes glows at night.

• Troll Peaks, a place in Norway, has massive stone crags that are said to be armies of trolls that were still fighting when the sun rose and turned them to stone.

• It is said that trolls hate noise and can be kept safely out of a town by ringing the church bells at night. They can also be kept away with branches of mistletoe, hung at the door of a home or the gate of a field.

• Despite their stupidity, trolls are the blacksmiths of the fairy world, experts in the art of metalwork. They are also known for their skills with magic and herbs.

Typhon

HANDS
He has snakes for hands as well: their wriggling bodies curl and grip onto mountain-sized rocks to hurl down to Earth.

HEAD
Typhon has the head of a dragon and a hundred other dragon or serpent heads spitting venom at his shoulders.

LEGS
Ordinary legs are not enough for a monster of this kind. Instead, he walks on many writhing viper legs.

WEAPONS
It is said that rivers of lava, storms of fire, and red-hot stones pour from his open mouth, and venom oozes from his eyes.

Typhon is one of the largest and most monstrous creatures in Greek and Roman mythology. He was tall enough to tower over mountains, his head brushing the skies. He is basically human in form, but has snakes and dragons for legs and hands, with a hundred vicious heads—some say serpents, others say lions, leopards, bulls, and boars. He is known as the Father of all Monsters. The gods feared him so much they fled from Olympus to Egypt.

ACTUAL SIZE

◄— 3 MILES (5 KM) —►

Athena, goddess of wisdom, persuaded the gods to return to Mount Olympus, where Zeus had to fight against Typhon. The monster cut muscles from the hands and feet of the mighty god and set his evil sister to guard them. But the gods tricked her and returned the muscles to Zeus. Finally, Typhon tore up Mount Etna and hurled it at Zeus. Zeus threw thunder and lightning at the mountain, casting it back on top of Typhon. Typhon remains trapped under Mount Etna today, erupting fire and lava through the top.

WHERE IN THE WORLD?

SICILY   GREECE

Typhon fought off Zeus at Mount Olympus in Greece but fled to Mount Etna in Sicily, where he met his end.

DID YOU KNOW?

• Even in his death throes, Typhon was able to father his own children, creating them from the bits of his body that were torn off by the thunder and lightning bolts cast by Zeus.

• Typhon's children were monstrous, and included the Nemean lion, Orthrus the two-headed dog, Cerberus the three-headed dog, the Chimera, and the Sphinx.

• Typhon's partner was the hideous Echidna, who raised their children in a cave.

• In some tales, Typhon is not killed by the rocks of Mount Etna, but by Zeus's mighty lightning bolts that he flung here, there, and everywhere in his rage at being torn to pieces.

Ziz Bird

EYES
The Ziz's eyes glow like lanterns, making the bird look as if he is lit from within.

WINGS
His wingspan is so great that it slowly covers the sun every evening. The immense wings enable him to flap quickly and quietly across the world.

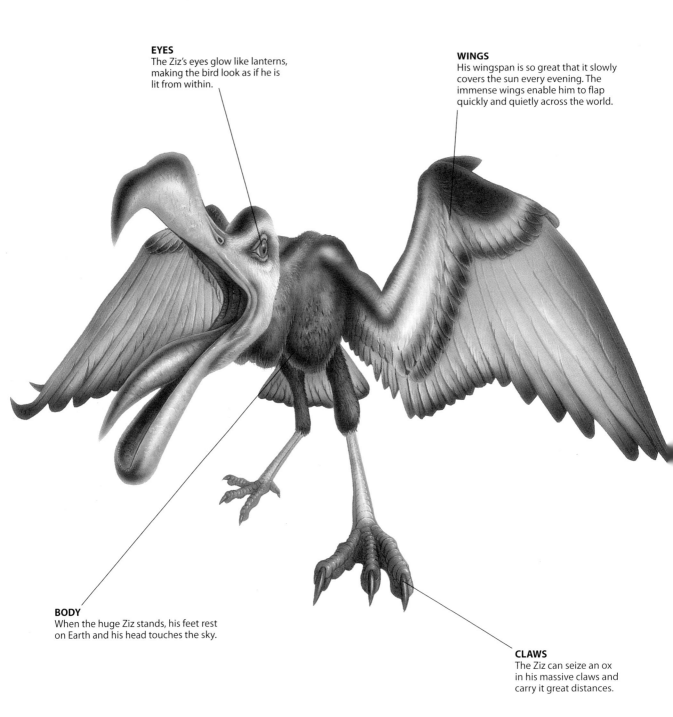

BODY
When the huge Ziz stands, his feet rest on Earth and his head touches the sky.

CLAWS
The Ziz can seize an ox in his massive claws and carry it great distances.

On the fifth day of creation, God made the gigantic Ziz bird and ordered him to use his tremendous wings to shade the Earth and protect it from storms. The Ziz's enormous size was such a hazard that God instructed him to fly high above the Earth. As king of the birds, he is responsible for protecting all flying, feathered creatures. A group of people spotted the Ziz standing in water up to its ankles with its head touching the sky. The people did not understand how large the Ziz was and assumed it was safe to swim there. They were warned that the water the Ziz stands in is so deep that an ax dropped in it seven days ago still had not reached the bottom.

 The Ziz swooped down on a shepherd's livestock one day and sunk his mighty claws into the back of an ox. As the Ziz lifted the ox off the ground, the shepherd grabbed the ox's leg and was carried away, too. The Ziz transported the ox and the shepherd far away and dropped them on top of a tower high above the sea. Later, when the Ziz returned to feast upon the ox, the shepherd cleverly tied ropes to the bird's legs so that he could hitch a ride with the Ziz away from the isolated tower.

WHERE IN THE WORLD?

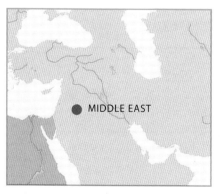

MIDDLE EAST

Hebraic mythology of the Middle East states that the Ziz flies around the world to protect every bird in creation.

ACTUAL SIZE

DID YOU KNOW?

• The Ziz was fashioned by God out of marshy ground along with all the other birds of the Earth.

• Once, a Ziz egg fell to the ground and broke. The fluid from the egg flooded several cities and crushed 300 cedar trees.

• The Ziz bird's presence reminds everyone to handle the forces of Earth with respect and care.

Azhi Dahaka

Area: Iran

Features: Part dragon, part snake; three heads, each with piercing eyes, gruesome teeth, and a forked tongue; terrible tail

Camazotz

Area: Mexico, Guatemala

Features: Body of a man, face and wings of a bat; huge ears; bat claws for toes; wears typical Mayan clothing and neck jewelry

Cthulhu

Area: Deep beneath the Pacific Ocean

Features: Made of alien matter; rubbery body covered in scales; tentacles around its lower jaw; giant claws on hands and feet; tiny wings

Cyclops

Area: Thrace, Mount Etna, Lycia, Lemnos, Crete, Mycenae, Tiryns

Features: One huge eye in the center of its forehead; pointed teeth; claws instead of nails on hands and feet; strong, muscular arms

Fomorian

Area: Ireland

Features: Huge eye in the center of its forehead; green, slimy skin that oozes poisonous sweat; mix of animal and human body parts; may be missing limbs or have multiple arms or legs

Frankenstein's Monster

Area: Switzerland

Features: Made of body parts taken from graves; thin, yellow skin; glowing, yellow eyes

Gargantua

Area: France

Features: Fist that could hold herds of cattle; had to ride a horse as big as six elephants

Gogmagog

Area: Southampton, Totnes in Britain

Features: Almost 13 feet tall; wild hair; piggy eyes; clothed in animal skins; shook the ground with his steps

Golem

Area: Eastern Europe

Features: Often looks like its creator; has a magic word on its forehead, which gives it life; tough, hard skin; grows bigger and stronger every day

Grendel

Area: Geatland

Features: Human weapons cannot harm him or break his skin; claws as hard as steel; sharp, unbreakable teeth; oversized, heavy head; fiery light in his eyes

Kronos

Area: Greece, Crete

Features: Lived to be hundreds of years old; uses a sickle; Zeus's father

Leviathan

Area: All the world's oceans

Features: Long, serpentine body; powerful neck and chest; jaws lined with rows of teeth; tough scales

Mongolian Death Worm

Area: Gobi Desert in Mongolia

Features: Blood red; about two feet long and as thick as a man's arm; it may have legs or hairs that help it move; jaws filled with fangs

Roc

Area: Iran, Pakistan, Madagascar

Features: Bird with a 48-foot (15-m) wingspan; each eye is bigger than a person's head; huge, sharp claws; hooked, pointed bill with dagger-like teeth

Shelob

Area: Mordor

Features: Spider demon with a thick hide; powerful jaws; needle-like barbs inject poison into a victim; hairs on her legs detect movement; spins rope-like webs

Talos

Area: Crete

Features: Made of bronze; the height of 50 men; weak spot is his heel

Thunderbird

Area: North America

Features: Two heads; hooked beak; huge, curved talons; powerful wings with long feathers; lightning flashes when it opens its eyes

Troll

Area: Scandinavia

Features: Ugly; small head and brain; sharp teeth and claws; strong

Typhon

Area: Sicily, Greece

Features: Dragon's head; man's body; dragons and serpents for arms, legs, and hands; eyes ooze venom

Ziz Bird

Area: Middle East

Features: When standing, its feet touch the Earth and its head touches the sky; eyes glow like lanterns; wingspan covers the sun; massive claws

Glossary

barb: a sharp point

brandish: to wave in a violent way

carnage: many deaths in one battle

echolocation: using sound waves to locate objects

frenzy: wild activity

impale: to use a pointed object to push through something

menace: a bully

ominous: warns that trouble is coming

pectoral: on the chest of an animal

primeval: of a very early time in history

puncture: to use something sharp to create a hole

rampant: uncontrolled

regurgitate: to throw up

rife: more than enough

shackle: a band that circles wrists or ankles and does not allow them to move

sinew: the matter connecting muscle to bone

taper: to get narrower

vigorous: working hard with spirit

writhe: to twist and turn in pain or to free oneself

For More Information

Books

Ganeri, Anita. *Giants and Ogres.* New York, NY: PowerKids Press, 2011.

Junbman, Ann. *The Prince Who Thought He Was a Rooster and Other Jewish Stories.* London, England: Frances Lincoln Publishers, 2007.

Rex, Adam. *Frankenstein Makes a Sandwich.* Orlando, FL: Harcourt, 2006.

Rumford, James. *Beowulf, a Hero's Tale Retold.* Boston, MA: Houghton Mifflin Books for Children, 2007.

Shelley, Mary Wollstonecraft. *Frankenstein.* Retold by Michael Bugan. Minneapolis, MN: Stone Arch Books, 2008.

Web Sites

Cryptozoology
www.yourdiscovery.com/paranormal/cryptozoology/index.shtml
Learn more about the Mongolian Death Worm and other creatures these special researchers try to find.

Giant Monsters
animal.discovery.com/convergence/giantmonsters/giantmonsters.html
Explore information and pictures of giant animals of the past.

Giants
www.theoi.com/greek-mythology/giants.html
Read more about the giants of Greek mythology.

World Myths and Legends in Art
www.artsmia.org/world-myths/
See how myths and legends are used in the art collection at the Minneapolis Institute of Art.

Publisher's note to educators and parents: Our editors have carefully reviewed these Web sites to ensure that they are suitable for students. Many Web sites change frequently, however, and we cannot guarantee that a site's future contents will continue to meet our high standards of quality and educational value. Be advised that students should be closely supervised whenever they access the Internet.

Index